FUN WITH MATH

Measurements

by Janie Scheffer

BLASTOFF! READERS 2

BLASTOFF! READERS, AN IMPRINT OF BELLWETHER MEDIA BY FLUTTERBEE

Blastoff! Readers are carefully developed by literacy experts to build reading stamina and move students toward fluency by combining standards-based content with developmentally appropriate text.

Level 1 provides the most support through repetition of high-frequency words, light text, predictable sentence patterns, and strong visual support.

Level 2 offers early readers a bit more challenge through varied sentences, increased text load, and text-supportive special features.

Level 3 advances early-fluent readers toward fluency through increased text load, less reliance on photos, advancing concepts, longer sentences, and more complex special features.

★ Blastoff! Universe

This edition first published in 2027 by Bellwether Media, Inc.

Library of Congress Cataloging-in-Publication Data

Names: Scheffer, Janie, 1992- author
Title: Measurements / by Janie Scheffer.
Description: Blastoff! readers. | Minneapolis, Minnesota : Bellwether Media, Inc, 2027. | Series: Fun with math | Includes bibliographical references and index. | Audience: Ages 5-8 | Audience: Grades 2-3 | Summary: "Relevant images match informative text in this introduction to measurements. Intended for students in kindergarten through third grade"--Provided by publisher
Identifiers: LCCN 2026011073 (print) | LCCN 2026011074 (ebook) | ISBN 9798898800529 library binding | ISBN 9798898802936 paperback | ISBN 9798898801762 ebook
Subjects: LCSH: Measurement | Weights and measures
Classification: LCC QA465 .S345 2027 (print) | LCC QA465 (ebook) | DDC 530.8--dc23/eng/20260319
LC record available at https://lccn.loc.gov/2026011073
LC ebook record available at https://lccn.loc.gov/2026011074

Editor: Rebecca Sabelko Designer: Brittany McIntosh

Printed in the United States of America, North Mankato, MN.

Table of Contents

What Are Measurements?

It is time to walk to the bus stop. I wonder how warm it is outside.

Do I need a coat?
I look at a **thermometer**.

How Warm Is It Outside?

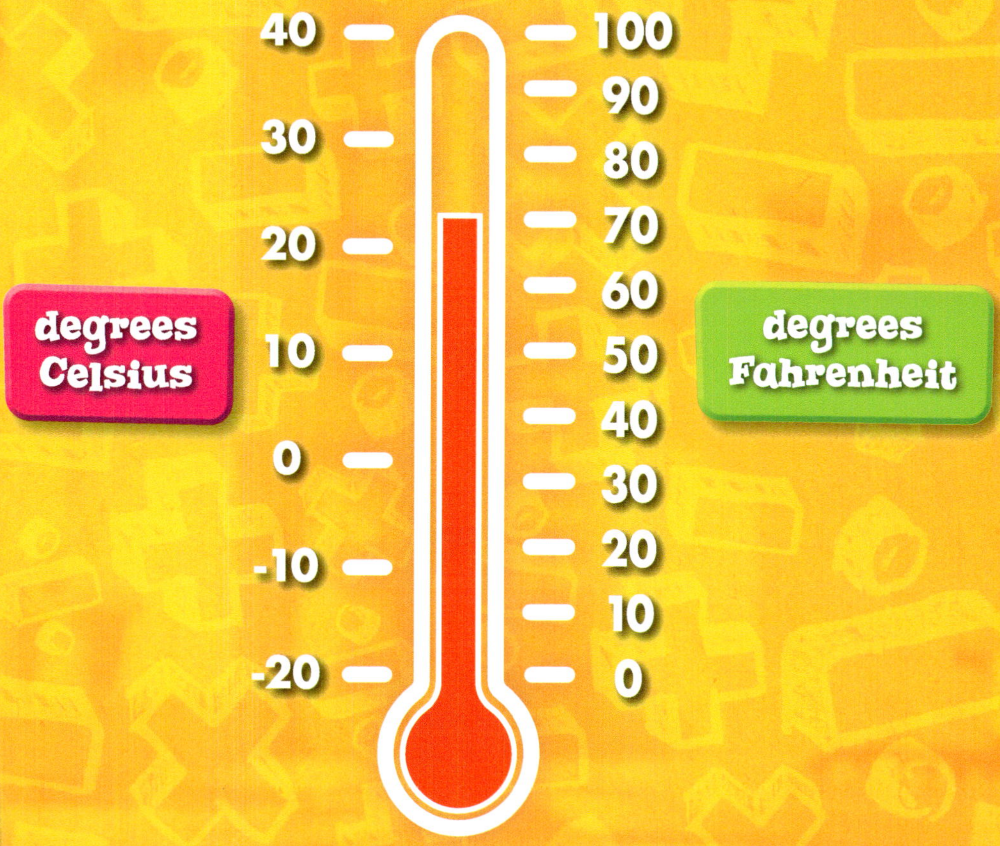

See answer on page 23!

Measurements give numbers to things. They tell about size and weight.

Measurements also show time, **temperature**, and amount.

People use **units** such as inches or cups to name exact measurements.

Other measurements are based on **estimates**.

People use measurements every day!

Measurements help people record **information** and **compare** things. They explain things too.

Working with Measurements

People often use tools to find measurements.

Rulers, clocks, **scales**, and thermometers help find these numbers.

What Is It?

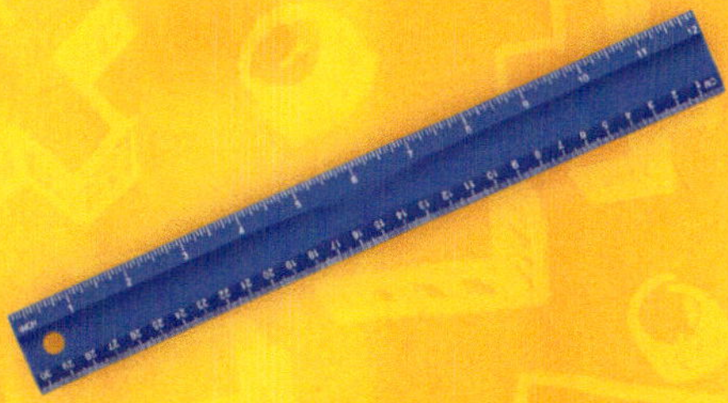

ruler

scale

clock

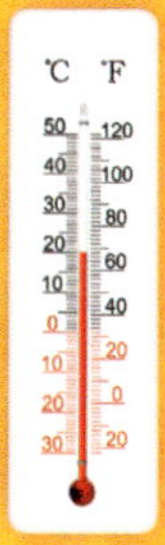

thermometer

People use rulers and tape measures to find the sizes of things. These tools measure length, **width**, and **height**.

They help us build things.

Scales measure weight. They show how heavy something is.

Clocks show time. People measure time in seconds, minutes, and hours.

Thermometers measure how hot or cold something is.

People use thermometers to find the temperature of food. Thermometers also show how hot or cold it is outside.

Measurements help people understand things in the world. They allow people to share information. They make things safer.

Measurements help people every day!

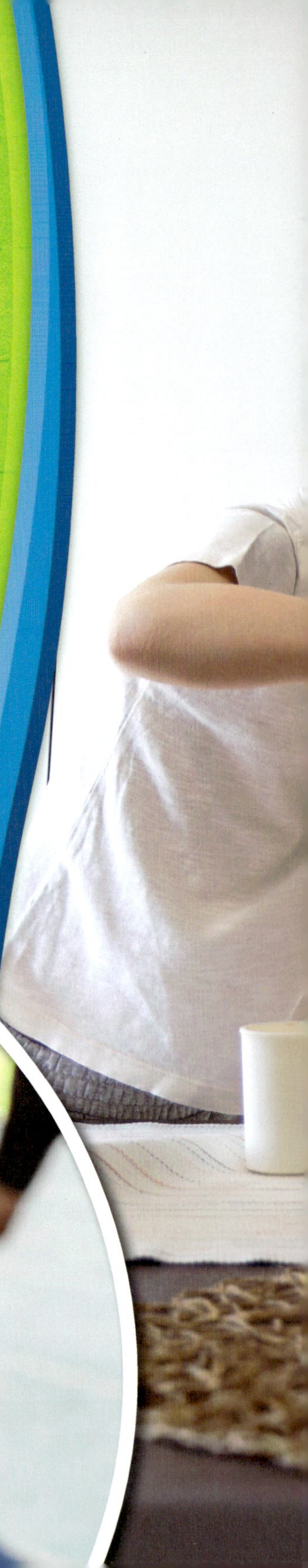

Glossary

compare–to show how things are alike or different

estimates–guesses about the amount, size, or value of something

height–the measurement of something from bottom to top

information–facts and knowledge

rulers–straight pieces of wood, metal, or plastic that are marked off in inches or other units and are used for measuring length

scales–tools used to measure weight

temperature–a measurement of how hot or cold something is

thermometer–a tool used to measure temperature

units–amounts or items used in measurements

width–the measurement of something from side to side

To Learn More

AT THE LIBRARY

Downs, Mike. *A Treasure of Measures.* San Francisco, Calif.: Chronicle Books, 2024.

Parsons, Michelle. *Luke's Flying Start.* New York, N.Y.: Kane Press, 2023.

Scheffer, Janie. *Time.* Minneapolis, Minn.: Bellwether Media, 2027.

ON THE WEB

FACTSURFER

Factsurfer.com gives you a safe, fun way to find more information.

1. Go to www.factsurfer.com.

2. Enter "measurements" into the search box and click .

3. Select your book cover to see a list of related content.

The thermometer on page 5 shows it is 70 degrees Fahrenheit (21 degrees Celsius)!

Index

The images in this book are reproduced through the courtesy of: Rose Nunez Smith, front cover; Elizabeth A. Cummings, p. 3; monkeybusinessimages, p. 4; DimaBerlin, p. 6; Ekkasit A Siam, p. 7; AndromedaPhotographer, p. 8; Ciricvelibor, pp. 8-9; InesBazdar, p. 10; Tada Images, p. 11; Westock Productions, p. 12; karen roach, p. 13 (ruler); Enes Altin Design, p. 13 (scale); RilakkuMaxx, p. 13 (clock); Tomas Ragina, p. 13 (thermometer); Dani Llao Calvet, p. 14; peopleimages.com, pp. 14-15; Daisy Daisy, p. 16; chomplearn, p. 17; Alohafalaminggo, p. 18; 4kodiak, p. 19; PeopleImages, p. 20; Ira.foto.2024, pp. 20-21; New Africa, p. 22.